MUSIC THROUGH TIME

Pauline Hall & Paul Harris

Piano Book 1

CONTENTS

MUSIC DEPARTMENT

OXFORD
UNIVERSITY PRESS

1638
Daphne

Anne Cromwell's Virginal Book
(17th century)

Covent Garden, the home of a famous market, was built in central London. It now has many interesting shops and an opera house, and is well worth a visit.

Anne Cromwell was a cousin of Oliver Cromwell and a keen amateur musician. She made a collection of short pieces, many of which were arrangements of popular tunes of the day.

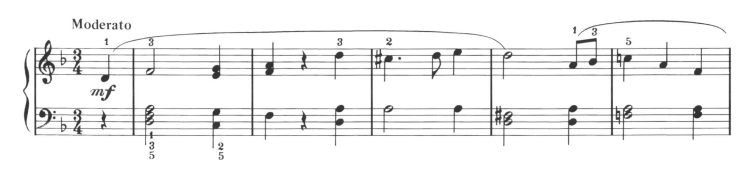

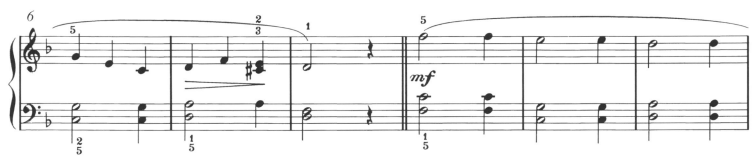

Printed in Great Britain

OXFORD UNIVERSITY PRESS, MUSIC DEPARTMENT, GREAT CLARENDON STREET, OXFORD OX2 6DP

Following the end of the English Civil War in 1649, Oliver Cromwell set up the Protectorate Parliament. Christmas was banned under their puritanical rule, as were entertainments like singing and dancing. Also in this year, the Dutch astronomer Huygens discovered the rings around the planet Saturn.

Lully was a composer and dancer at the court of King Louis XIV of France. Louis was a keen dancer and part of Lully's job was to provide the King with dance music, like this piece.

1655
Minuet

Jean-Baptiste Lully
(1632–87)

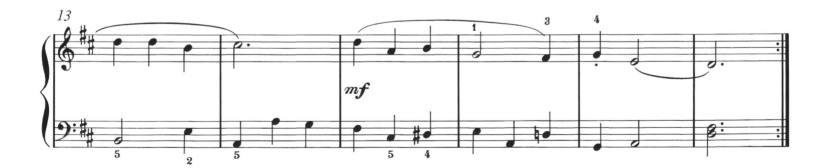

1689
Minuet

Henry Purcell
(1659–95)

William of Orange and his wife Mary were crowned
King and Queen of England, Scotland, and Ireland.
They accepted a Bill of Rights, which led to a
weakening of the power of the monarchy.

Purcell was one of the greatest English composers.
One of his most famous works is the opera *Dido and
Aeneas*, first performed at a girls' boarding school.

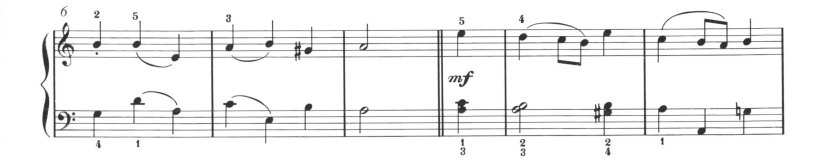

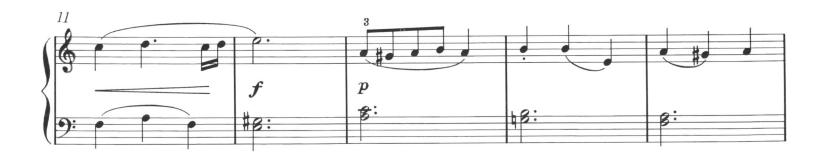

The Great Northern War broke out with Denmark, Russia, and Poland on one side, and Sweden on the other. Sweden lost its empire, and Russia became a powerful nation for the first time, under Peter the Great.

Jeremiah Clarke began his musical life as a boy chorister at the Chapel Royal, later returning as organist. This is probably his most famous piece, although it was once thought to be by Purcell. Clarke shot himself in 1707 after an unhappy love affair—though one newspaper of the day said it was because the organ at St Paul's Cathedral was flat!

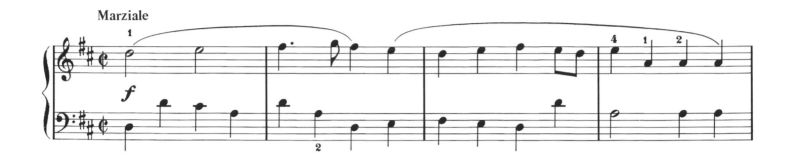

1768
March

William Boyce
(1711–79)

The explorer Captain James Cook charted the coasts of New Zealand and eastern Australia in his ship HMS *Endeavour* during his first journey round the world. The *Encyclopaedia Britannica* was first published in weekly parts, of which 100 were planned—today it fills 29 volumes, each over an inch thick.

This March was part of an Overture to *The Ode for his Majesty's Birthday*. It was part of Boyce's duties to compose these every year—first for George II and later for George III. Boyce is buried under the dome of St Paul's Cathedral, where he began his musical career as a choirboy.

The 'Boston Tea Party' took place, when American revolutionaries threw vast quantities of tea into Boston harbour rather than paying the British taxes on it. John Broadwood made the first square piano, and the waltz became popular in Vienna.

Haydn has been called 'the father of the Symphony'—he wrote over 100! If his life was comparatively uneventful, his vast output of music contains surprises in almost every piece.

Franz Joseph Haydn
(1732–1809)

1779
Arioso

Wolfgang Amadeus Mozart
(1756–91)

Captain Cook, on his third voyage to the Pacific this year, was killed by natives on the island of Hawaii. The world's first all-iron bridge was built across the River Severn in Coalbrookdale, Shropshire.

An Arioso is a short tuneful piece, rather like a song. Mozart began composing at the age of 5, and by the time he was 12 he had written his first opera!

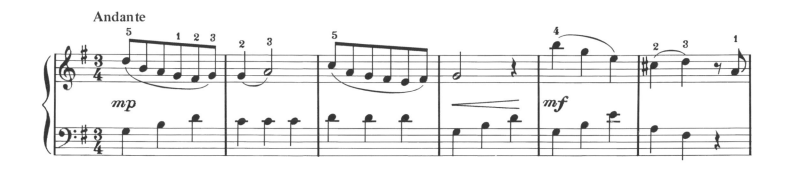

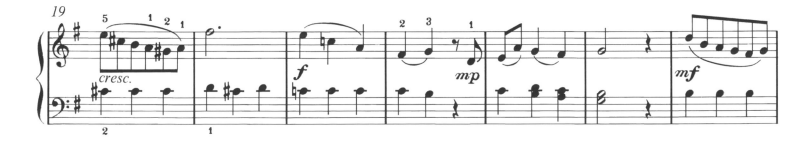

The British doctor Edmund Jenner used an eight-year-old boy as a human guinea-pig for the first smallpox vaccination. Luckily for both of them, the experiment was a success.

James Hook was an English composer and organist who composed over 200 songs.

1796
Gavotta

James Hook
(1746–1827)

Allegro moderato

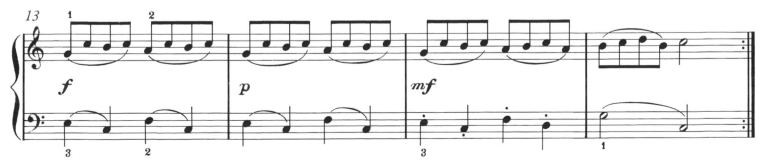

1799
Swinging Along

During Napoleon's occupation of Egypt, a French soldier discovered the Rosetta Stone—a black stone tablet bearing inscriptions which provided the key to deciphering ancient Egyptian writings. It is now kept in the British Museum.

Wenzel Müller
(1767–1835)

Wenzel Müller was a prolific Austrian composer and conductor. He wrote over 200 operettas for the theatre, where he had begun his career as a violinist at the age of fifteen, but today is only known for his easy piano pieces.

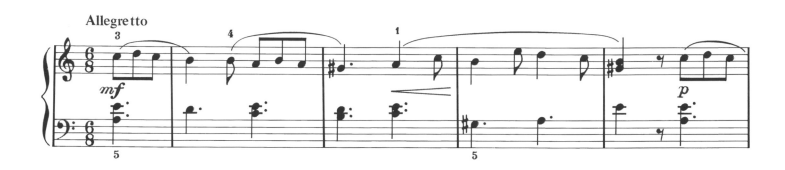

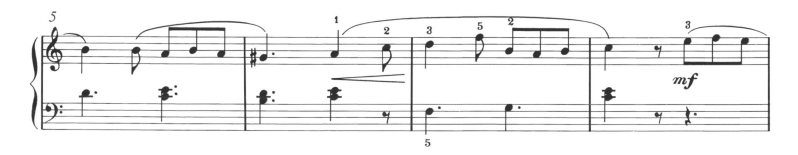

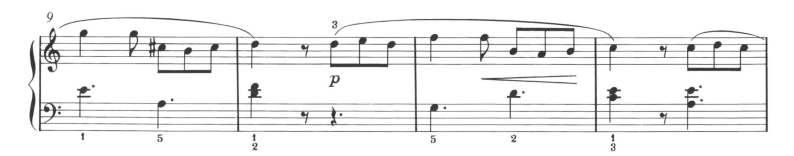

Napoleon Bonaparte was voted Consul for life by the French people. In London, Thomas Wedgewood and Humphrey Davy took the first photograph; the image quickly faded, though—photography still had a long way to go!

Weber, a German composer, conductor, and pianist, travelled widely and held many posts including one at the court in Stuttgart from which he was banished because of suspected embezzlement! *Écossaise* is the French for 'Scottish Dance', though the name is rather a mystery since there's nothing obviously Scottish in the character of many such pieces.

1802
Écossaise

Carl Maria von Weber
(1786–1826)

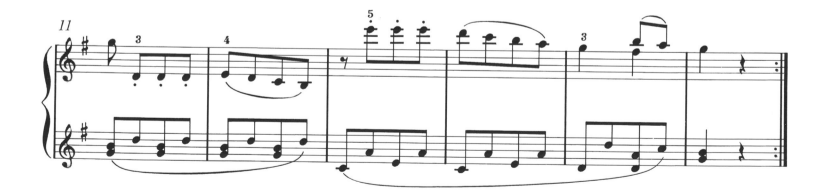

1810
Allegro

Johann Hässler
(1747–1822)

The composer Schumann was born in this year. Initially he was just as interested in books, champagne, and girlfriends as in music, but he soon gave up a career in law for one as a pianist. However, he damaged his hand by using a mechanical device designed to strengthen it—a warning to all those inclined to over-practise!

Hässler was a German composer and pianist. He lived and worked in Moscow for much of his life, enjoying considerable popularity there, and wrote a vast amount of keyboard music.

After using a rolled-up piece of paper in 1809, the composer Louis Spohr introduced the baton for orchestral conducting, to the orchestra's initial alarm but ultimate approval. Blind and mad, George III died aged 81—one of the longest reigning British monarchs. Washington Irving wrote the children's tale *Rip Van Winkle*.

Thomas Attwood was an English composer who became a favourite pupil of Mozart and later a friend of Mendelssohn, who dedicated several works to him.

Thomas Attwood
(1765–1838)

1823
Ländler

Franz Schubert
(1797–1828)

Charles Macintosh developed a new fabric for making raincoats; though waterproof, the material was found to give off a nasty smell in the summer heat. The game of rugby was invented when William Webb Ellis, a pupil at Rugby School, picked up the ball and ran with it during a football game.

Apparently, one of Schubert's favourite haunts was a Viennese coffee-house frequented by Beethoven. The timid Schubert would sit gazing reverently at the figure of the great man alone in the corner. A *ländler* is a type of slow waltz which originated in Landel, a part of Austria.

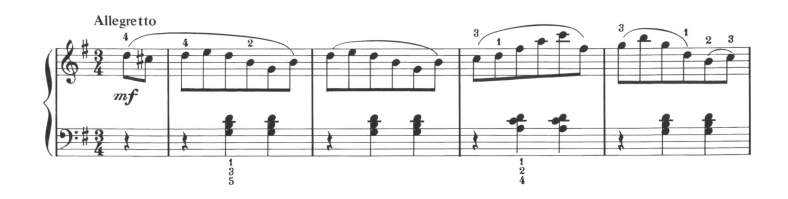

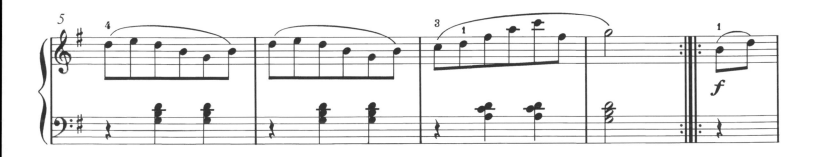

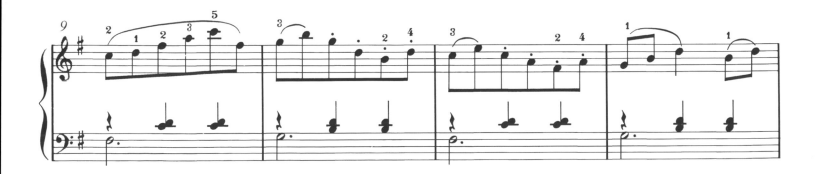

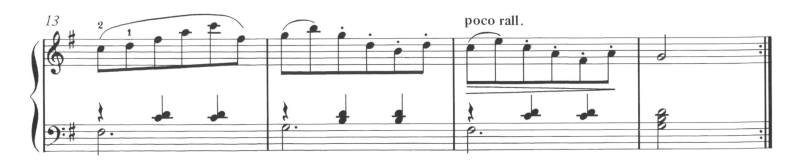

The concertina was patented by Sir Charles Wheatstone, and a new instrument, the mouth organ, arrived in Vienna from China! George Stephenson built his famous steam locomotive *The Rocket*, and the first Oxford and Cambridge University Boat Race was won by Oxford.

Rossini had a varied childhood—singing in churches, playing harpsichord in theatres, and being apprenticed to a blacksmith! *William Tell* was his last opera, although he lived for a further 40 years. Tell was a famous Swiss folk hero, best known for shooting an arrow through an apple resting on his son's head.

1835
Spring Morning

William Crotch
(1775–1847)

William Henry Fox Talbot took the earliest negative photograph, of his house in Wiltshire. Hans Christian Anderson wrote his fairy stories.

William Crotch was a sort of English Mozart—a child prodigy who gave organ recitals in London at the age of four! He went on to become the first principal of the Royal Academy of Music when it opened in 1822.

At Lourdes in south-west France a fourteen-year-old peasant girl called Bernadette claimed to have seen a miraculous vision of the Virgin Mary surrounded by light. Lourdes is now a world-famous place of pilgrimage.

The Galop was a type of ballroom dance. This one, better known as the 'Can-can', is from *Orpheus in the Underworld*, the most popular of Offenbach's 90 operettas. His works were followed by those of Johann Strauss, Arthur Sullivan, and Franz Lehár, and ultimately led to the twentieth-century musical.

1858
Galop

Jacques Offenbach
(1819–80)

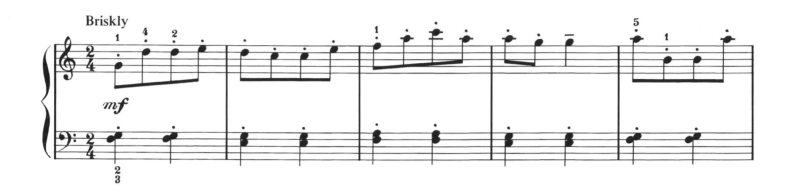

1865
Andantino

Felix Le Couppey
(1811–87)

Oxford mathematician Charles Dodgson wrote *Alice's Adventures in Wonderland* under the name of Lewis Carroll. The American Civil War ended on 9 April when the Southern Confederate forces surrendered to the Northern Union. Six days later, Abraham Lincoln was assassinated in a Washington theatre by John Wilkes Booth, a failed actor.

Felix Le Couppey was a French pianist and composer. He taught at the Paris Conservatoire for over 60 years.

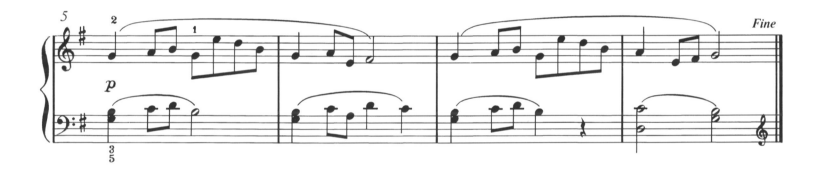

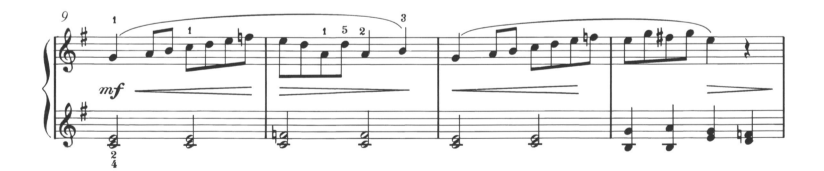

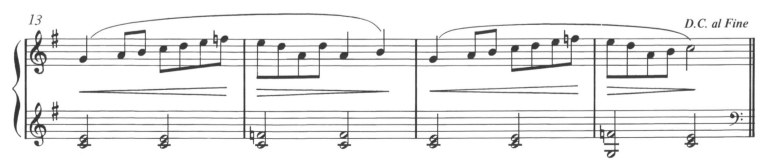

In London, the first medical school for women was founded and the first roller-skating rink was opened. In Brooklyn, USA, chewing gum was invented. Captain Matthew Webb became the first person to swim the English Channel—it took him 21 hours 45 minutes.

This tune is from one of the world's most popular operas, *Carmen*, first produced this year. Amazingly, it was coolly received and criticized as 'tuneless'. Bizet died shortly afterwards, never knowing the great success it was to achieve.

Toreador's Song

Georges Bizet
(1838–75)

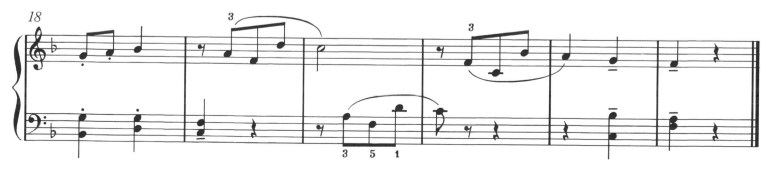

1883
Legend

The Orient Express train made its first journey from Paris to Istanbul. In America, W. F. Cody—otherwise known as 'Buffalo Bill'—organized a touring 'Wild West Show', later including the Sioux Indian chief Sitting Bull. Other famous Wild West figures living at this time included Billy the Kid, Jesse James, and Wyatt Earp.

Pyotr Ilyich Tchaikovsky
(1840–93)

Tchaikovsky has always been one of the most popular composers. His music is tuneful, colourfully scored, and filled with emotion. He led something of a tormented life, and wrote that his whole life was spent 'regretting the past and hoping for the future, never being satisfied with the present'.

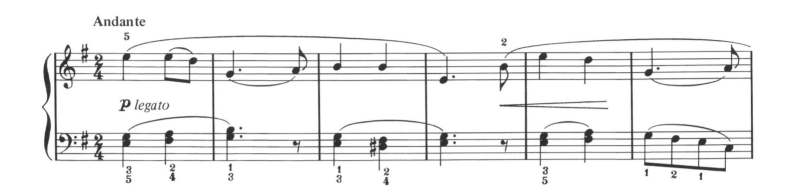

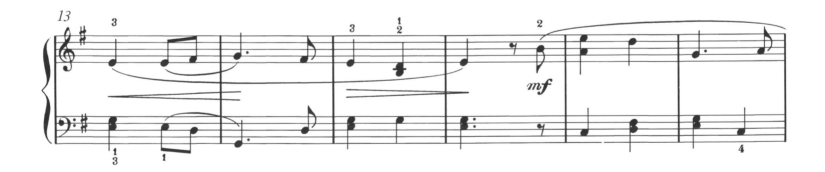

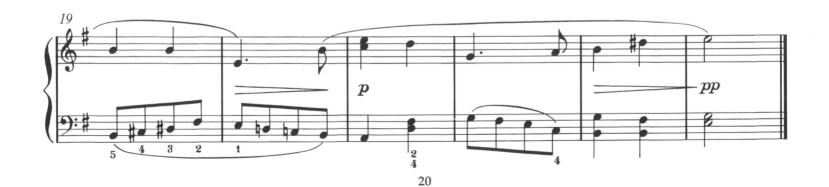

Night Journey

Cornelius Gurlitt
(1820–1901)

Emil Berliner recorded sound on a flat disc for the first time, using the trademark 'Gramophone'. A committee was formed to organize the modern Olympic Games, and Rudyard Kipling wrote *The Jungle Book*. The Blackpool Tower, a replica of the Eiffel Tower in Paris, was opened.

Cornelius Gurlitt was a German composer and keyboard player. He wrote three operas, though most of his compositions are for piano.

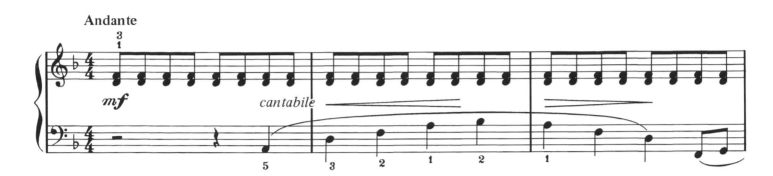

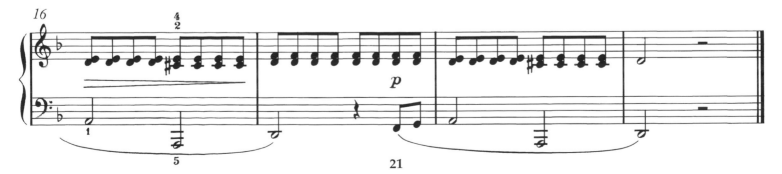

1901
The Easy Winners

Scott Joplin
(1868–1917)

Queen Victoria died after a reign of 63 years, aged 81. The first effective vacuum cleaner (it sucked, rather than blew) was invented by Hubert Booth. Marconi succeeded in sending the first transatlantic radio signal, the first motor-driven bicycle was made, and the first Nobel prizes were awarded.

Scott Joplin popularized the piano rag with his *Maple Leaf Rag*, initially turned down for publication as being too difficult. He always said that his rags should not be played too fast.

Charles Chaplin made his first film. The Suffragette Emily Davison died after throwing herself in front of the King's horse at the Derby, protesting for votes for women.

Satie, a French composer, was a somewhat eccentric character. He frequently gave his works unconventional titles, and developed a uniquely individual style. Among his unusual interests was collecting umbrellas.

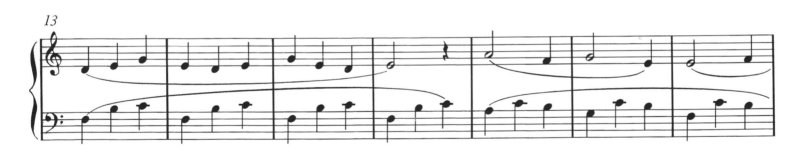

1950
Swaying

Soulima Stravinsky
(1910–)

China, which had become a Communist State the previous year, invaded Tibet. The Korean Civil War began, and India became an Independent Republic. Frank Loesser's musical *Guys and Dolls* was produced on Broadway in New York.

Soulima Stravinsky is the Swiss-born son of Igor Stravinsky—one of the major figures of twentieth-century music.

1950
Polka

Dimitry Kabalevsky
(1904–87)

Kabalevsky was a Russian composer and pianist who worked as a silent-movie pianist in his youth.

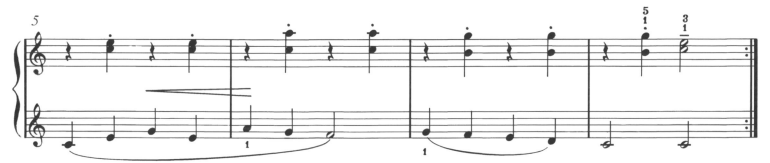

From Twenty-Four Easy Piano Pieces for Children, OP.39.

BBC 2 broadcast for the first time, and the 'Twist' was the latest dance craze to sweep Britain. The nine-year Vietnam War started, as the USA sent troops to support South Vietnam against the Communist North.

Robert Washburn is an American composer. Apart from many short pieces written for children, he has composed a number of large-scale works and often uses music that sounds 'Wild West' in style.

Shepherd's Song

Robert Washburn

(1928–)

1990
Dragonflies

Paul Harris
(1957–)

This piece has a light, airy quality which should remind you
of dragonflies. Try to convey this as you play it.

Paul Harris
(1957–)

Listen carefully to the spooky sounds you can create in
this piece. It will sound even more effective if you open
the lid of the piano.

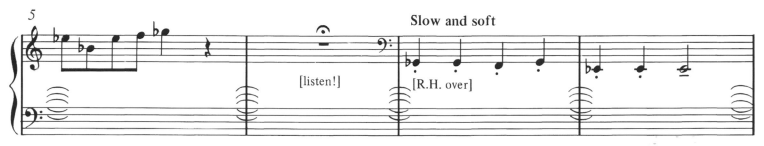

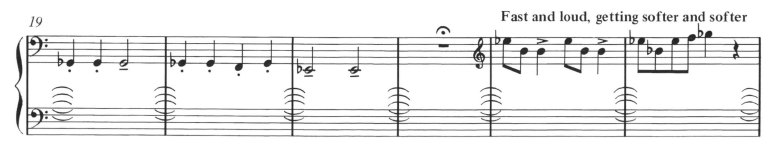

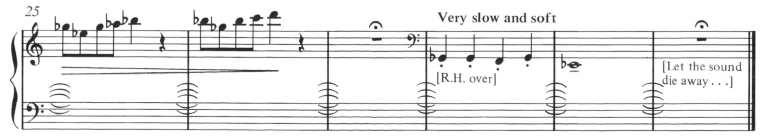

Reproduced and printed by
Halstan & Co. Ltd., Amersham, Bucks., England